D0742115

Hernandez, Roger E.
Early explorations :
the 1500s /
2008
33305 3149
gi   02/04/09

EARLY EXPLORATIONS

THE 1500s

BY
ROGER E. HERNÁNDEZ

Marshall Cavendish
Benchmark
New York

MARSHALL CAVENDISH BENCHMARK
99 WHITE PLAINS ROAD
TARRYTOWN, NEW YORK 10591-5502
www.marshallcavendish.us

Text copyright © 2009 by Marshall Cavendish Corporation

All rights reserved. No part of this book may be reproduced or utilized in any form or by any means electronic or mechanical including photocopying, recording, or by any information storage and retrieval system, without permission from the copyright holders.

All Web sites were available and accurate when this book was sent to press.

LIBRARY OF CONGRESS CATALOGING-IN-PUBLICATION DATA
Hernández, Roger E.
Early explorations : the 1500s / by Roger E. Hernández.
p. cm. — (Hispanic America)
Summary: "Provides comprehensive information on the history of Spanish exploration in the United States"—Provided by publisher. Includes index.
ISBN 978-0-7614-2937-1
1. America—Discovery and exploration—Spanish—Juvenile literature.
2. Southern States—Discovery and exploration—Spanish—Juvenile literature.
3. Southwest, New—Discovery and exploration—Spanish—Juvenile literature.
4. Spain—Colonies—America—History—Juvenile literature.
5. Explorers—America—Biography—Juvenile literature.
6. Explorers—Spain—Biography—Juvenile literature. I. Title. II. Series.
E123.H47 2008
970.01'6—dc22
2007026406

Photo research by Linda Sykes

Cover photo: The Granger Collection
Back cover photo: Private Collection/The Bridgeman Art Library

The photographs in this book are used by permission and through the courtesy of:
The Granger Collection: 1, 4, 10-11, 14, 16, 19, 20, 25, 30, 32, 35, 39, 51, 55, 57, 60, 62. Alamy: Cindy White, 7; Northwind Picture Archive, 22; Visions of America LLC, 47; Denita Delimont, 68; Mervyn Rees, 69; David Lyons, 71.? The Mariners Museum, Newport News, VA, 9.? Library of Congress: Rare Book Room, 27; Map Collection, 52.? The Bancroft Library, 23.? The Bridgeman Art Library: Private Collection, 36-37. ?National Geographic Image Collection: The British Library, 43.? Texas History Collection, Center for American History, 44-45, 66.? Pensacola Historical Society, 48.? Art Resource, NY: Galleria Nazionale della Sicilia, Palermo, Sicily, Italy/Scala, 54.? Warren Wilson College Archaeology: photo courtesy Robin Beck, David Moore and Christopher Rodning, 56.

EDITOR: Joy Bean   PUBLISHER: Michelle Bisson
ART DIRECTOR: Anahid Hamparian   SERIES DESIGNER: Kristen Branch

Printed in China
1 3 5 6 4 2

CONTENTS

CHAPTER ONE

THE SPANISH CAME

THE TRADITIONAL VIEW OF U.S. HISTORY SAYS the North American continent was settled by people of British ancestry. American students have long been taught about the first English colony, established in 1607 in Jamestown, Virginia, and about the Pilgrims' landing in 1620 near Plymouth Rock, Massachusetts. History says these colonies helped shape what would become the United States.

There is no doubt that those men and women and their descendants spread out from their original settlements in the Northeast. They carried with them the English language and the fundamentals of British society, modified by the conditions of life on the American frontier. Their culture and political traditions form the foundations of the United States, upon which immigrants from across the globe and enslaved Africans later made their own contributions.

Opposite:
The Spanish head for unexplored territories aboard their ship.

But the British were not the only Europeans in North America four hundred years ago. Spanish explorers came before them, just a few years after Columbus's first landing. Spain was at the time the most powerful nation on earth, and the influence of the Spanish people and their descendants on the United States can still be seen today.

For instance, states in the West and Southwest still carry the names given by *conquistadores* from Spain, explorers who were among the first Europeans in North America. Colorado, which means red, got its name because of the reddish color of the muddy Colorado River. Montana was named for its mountainous landscape. New Mexico was the region Spaniards settled after conquering "old" Mexico. Nevada means snowfall. Historians are uncertain how California received its name, but one belief is that it is named for an island featured in the 1510 novel *Las Sergas de Esplandián,* which was popular at the time. Historians are also unsure of how Texas got its name. Some say Texas is a Native-American word meaning friend, and others say it originates from the Spanish spelling, Tejas, which means roofing tiles.

Those states, as well as parts of other regions, were once part of a Spanish empire that governed much of what is now the United States. Spain ruled territories in North America for nearly three hundred years, longer than the United States has been an independent republic. In some areas, especially in the small towns near the

The name Texas may have come from the homes in the area, which were made with red-tiled (Tejas) roofs. These roofs still dot the landscape of Texas.

Sangre de Cristo Mountains in northern New Mexico, there still live people with Spanish surnames who are not recent immigrants but claim descent from the original Spanish settlers who lived there as far back as the early 1600s. They say that their families have lived in the Southwest longer than the families who descend from the Pilgrims have lived in New England.

Other Hispanics, including recent immigrants, also point proudly to the old Spanish colonial legacy. They live in Spanish-named cities and towns of every size in many states, from tiny Hernandez in New Mexico to midsized Amarillo (which means yellow) in Texas.

Los Angeles, California was originally named El Pueblo de Nuestra Señora la Reina de los Ángeles Sobre el Río

Porciuncula, or The Town of Our Lady Queen of the Angels on the Porciuncula River. The city was named in 1781 by Spanish settlers from the nearby *mission* of San Gabriel Arcángel. This is one of dozens of churches, forts, and government buildings in Arizona, California, New Mexico, and Texas built by Spanish colonists that still stand today, physical reminders of the Spanish presence in the United States. Their architecture has influenced countless Mediterranean-style housing developments and public buildings constructed in recent years across the country. The Spanish influence is particularly strong in the old Spanish dominions of California, the Southwest, and Florida.

Florida too was once controlled by the Spanish. In fact, it was ruled by the Spanish before any other place in the United States. In 1513 the explorer Juan Ponce de León became the first European known to have set foot on the North American continent. He named it Florida, historians say, because of the many flowers he saw in bloom and because he landed on the day of Pascua Florida, known as Easter Sunday. After exploring other parts of the world, Ponce de Léon returned eight years later to try to establish a permanent colony near present-day Tampa. He died in the effort, killed by a Native-American's arrow. That did not discourage fellow Spanish explorer Pánfilo de Narváez, who in 1528 made a similar attempt at colonization in the same general area of Florida's Gulf Coast. In pursuit of gold, he left a trail of dead and tortured Native

Americans from Tampa to coastal Texas, but he too died before establishing a lasting colony.

The Spanish explored places farther north than Florida, even though they did not settle there or leave any buildings known to have survived. Although few people associate Spanish exploration with Canada or New England, around 1524 a Portuguese explorer who worked for Spain named Esteban Gómez mapped the northeastern seaboard, in what would one day be the United States. Something similar happened on the other side of the continent. Juan Rodríguez Cabrillo became the first European to navigate the coast of California, and Juan de Fuca explored the Pacific coast of Washington State. Although neither voyage resulted in a permanent settlement, the Strait of Juan de Fuca and the San Juan Islands are reminders of the explorers from long ago.

In pursuit of gold, Pánfilo de Narváez made an attempt at colonizing Florida.

Gómez, de Fuca, and Cabrillo are among the lesser-known explorers of the 1500s. More famous are Hernando de Soto, Francisco Vázquez de Coronado, and Álvar Núñez Cabeza de Vaca. Cabeza de Vaca's story is perhaps the most remarkable. After surviving a shipwreck in 1528 as part of the Narváez expedition, he had to forget about the riches that motivated most conquistadores and concentrate just on staying alive. He spent the next six years walking from coastal Louisiana to Mexico, barefoot, sometimes a slave of Native Americans. Still, Cabeza de Vaca developed friendly relationships with the Native Americans. This was unusual among the conquistadores, men whose actions remain controversial today. Even as they brought Western ideas to the areas they explored, they conquered those areas with much bloodshed and abuse of Native Americans.

The aim of de Soto's and Coronado's exploration was to become rich by finding gold—but also to find trades routes. De Soto landed in Florida in 1539 in pursuit of the precious metal and embarked on a three-year journey through what is now called the Deep South of the United States, from Georgia to the Mississippi River and as far west as Arkansas. Around the same time, Coronado was searching from New Mexico to Kansas for a legendary city of gold named Cíbola.

Cabeza de Vaca and his fellow Spanish sailors gather their things on the beach after their shipwreck.

None of those famed explorers succeeded in establishing permanent colonies. It was not until Pedro Menéndez de Avilés founded Saint Augustine, Florida, in 1565 that Spain established its first successful settlement in North America. Some thirty years later, near present-day Santa Fe, New Mexico, Juan de Oñate founded the first permanent settlement in the Southwest.

The Spanish colonial imprint is less visible in Florida than in the Southwest. Florida colonists left no communities of descendants as colonists did in New Mexico. The oldest Hispanic community in Florida is in Tampa and dates back to just the 1880s, when cigar makers emigrated from Cuba. An even larger community in Miami has its roots in the early 1960s, when Cubans began to flee the revolution led by Cuban president Fidel Castro. The architectural legacy of Spain is not readily visible in either area of Florida. In contrast to the Southwest, hardly any old Spanish colonial structures still stand—nearly all of the Mediterranean-style buildings in Florida were built within the last century, inspired by Spanish architecture but not built by Spanish colonists. Yet some original Spanish colonial architecture does survive in Florida. Foremost is Castillo de San Marcos, built to defend Saint Augustine, the oldest continuously occupied town of European origin in the United States. More Spanish structures may still be found in Northern regions. Archaeologists have begun to explore what they believe is a sixteenth-century Spanish settlement in the Appalachian Mountains of North Carolina, north of where historians thought Spain's northernmost outpost was located.

So by the time English colonists founded Jamestown, Spanish colonial settlements already existed in Florida and the Southwest. Their legacy forms part of the history of the United States.

CHAPTER TWO

FIRST STEPS

T HE SPANISH EXPLORATION OF WHAT IS NOW
the United States can be traced to October 12, 1492,
when Christopher Columbus, the Italian navigator led
a journey of discovery for Spain under King Ferdinand and
Queen Isabella. Columbus landed on one of the Bahamas, the
group of islands a few miles east of Florida. It was the discovery of America—a term contested by those who think the
native inhabitants had already discovered America when they
crossed a now-underwater land bridge over the *Bering Strait*
tens of thousands of years earlier.

Contrary to popular legend, Columbus was not trying to
prove the world was round. Educated people of his day were
already pretty sure it was a sphere. Instead, Columbus was
trying to reach the gold, silk, and spices of Asia by sailing

Opposite:
King Ferdinand
and Queen
Isabella of Spain
sent explorers to
discover new
areas of the
world.

west across the Atlantic Ocean, in the opposite direction European voyagers always took in those days. Explorers who took the eastern route had to travel over land, crossing huge deserts, or sail around Africa before heading east. This route had yielded riches to countries that had traversed it, such as Portugal, but the adventurers who dared make the long, perilous journey faced danger from Muslims and other rivals.

A portrait of Christopher Columbus.

Columbus figured he could avoid some of those risks and also make the trip shorter with his westward route. If the world was round, he thought, it did not matter whether somebody sailed east or west to get to the opposite side, because the ship would get there anyway. There was the danger of storms and unknown pirates, but geographically, at least, it was possible.

What nobody, including Columbus, expected was that there was a gigantic landmass blocking the path between Europe and Asia—what we now call North, Central, and South America. So when Columbus landed on that little Bahamian island, it was the first encounter between two populations utterly unaware of the existence of the other.

Although there may have been similar earlier encounters, they had not been documented. For instance, many historians believe the Vikings landed in America centuries before 1492. But those voyages, if they really did happen, changed little in the history of the world. Columbus's expedition, in contrast, eventually led to the creation of the United States, Canada, Mexico, Brazil—every single nation in the *Western Hemisphere*. And because of the important role some of those nations have played in the world, it can be argued that the landing of Columbus—perhaps like no other moment—marked the start of a new era in the history of humankind.

Columbus died in 1506, not knowing what he had discovered. He always thought he had landed in Asia. In the years that followed, people began to realize the Americas were not part of Asia, but rather two different continents, which in some parts were rich in treasure. Hearing about the new lands, Spaniards of all social classes sought to make their fortunes in the newly discovered lands. New expeditions were often led by younger members of the lower nobility whose family inheritance had gone to older brothers. They were lured in part by the gold they thought they would find and in part by the idea of spreading the Catholic faith. At least some parts of Spain had been ruled by Muslims since the year 711, but in 1492, the same year that Columbus landed in the new world, the last *Moorish* kingdom of Spain was conquered by Spanish Catholic armies.

The Spanish nation, full of lust for gold as well as religion, found its outlet in the New World. First, Spaniards conquered the islands of Hispaniola (1496), Puerto Rico (1508), and Cuba (1511). Their legacy lives on in the language and culture of Cuba, Puerto Rico, and the Dominican Republic (which makes up about two-thirds of Hispaniola). But the price in human suffering was high—the historian David Weber said that in Hispaniola only 30,000 Native Americans were still alive out of "a densely populated island when Columbus planted Spain's first New World colony."

PONCE DE LÉON'S FOUNTAIN OF YOUTH

One of those energetic young Spaniards with an equal mixture of adventurous courage, cruelty, religious zeal, and thirst for gold was Juan Ponce de León. Ponce de León was typical of the conquistadores. He was born into a proud but poor noble family. He fought in Spain's wars against the Moors. He even accompanied Columbus on the admiral's second voyage to the Americas. Ponce de León decided to make his fortune in the new lands as an *adelantado*. In pursuit of that effort he went further than most, as he rose to become governor of Puerto Rico and one of the wealthiest men in the Caribbean. But his major claim to fame is that he is regarded as the first European to have set foot in what is now the United States.

Some historians believe Spanish slave raiders had landed in Florida before Ponce de León but kept it quiet to avoid being caught by Spanish authorities, which forbade unauthorized Native-American slavery. One unconfirmed story even says that Ponce de Léon's group came across one Native American who could speak Spanish. But Ponce de León is the first European visitor for whom there is a definite record.

In March of 1513, with permission from the Spanish royal court, Ponce de León sailed north from Puerto Rico with three ships. He probably landed around what is today's Daytona Beach on Easter Sunday, April 2, 1513.

The ceremony in which Ponce de León took posses-sion of Florida in the name of the Spanish crown was very formal, with the reading of proclamations, the unfurling of flags, and the raising of Christian crosses. Of course, the Native Americans who had been living there did not understand what it was all about. And even if they did,

Juan Ponce de León is said to have been the first European to set foot in what is now the United States.

FOUNTAIN OF YOUTH OR SOURCE OF POWER?

Legend has it that Ponce de León went to Florida seeking the Fountain of Youth. The idea that magical waters existed that made old men young again was a powerful myth in medieval European tradition, but even back then many people scoffed at the notion of physical *rejuvenation*, knowing it was just a tall tale.

What about Ponce de Léon? Nobody knows for sure if he really thought he would find an actual source of water that could literally make people younger. Historians believe that perhaps the rebirth he sought was more symbolic. At the very least he wanted to gain back some of the status he had lost when he was ousted as governor of Puerto Rico in a political struggle won by the son of Columbus. If he found more gold, he figured, his power, wealth, and prestige would be reborn.

they were unlikely to want to be ruled by the strange, bearded newcomer.

Florida's original inhabitants quickly made their displeasure known. As the Spanish expedition sailed south along the coast, charting the rivers, inlets, bays, and other features of the coastline, they were attacked by Ais Indians at a small village near Cape Canaveral. The historian Weber said the Ais may have been "incited by earlier visits from Spanish slave hunters." Ponce de León and his men sailed on, continuing to make charts as they sailed along the coast and passed through the tricky waters around the Florida Keys with the help of a pilot named Antonio de Alaminos, an expert on sailing the Caribbean and nearby seas. Eventually they rounded the Dry Tortugas and turned north to explore the Gulf Coast of Florida, making it as far north as the area around Charlotte Harbor. They continued to map the region. Their charts and logs remain the first record of Florida's coastline.

In the Charlotte Harbor area Ponce de León stopped, perhaps at Estero Island, to repair his vessels and replenish his provisions. But he and his crew were attacked by Calusa Indians who, like the Ais, may have had earlier encounters with Spanish slave raiders. Ponce de León's men retreated to their ships. And, perhaps because of the ferocity of the attacks and their own decreasing strength, the explorers decided to head back to Puerto Rico and give up, for then, their dream of colonizing Florida or

When attacked by Native Americans, Ponce de León retreated to his ship.

even marching past the coast to search for gold.

After the failure of his expedition, Ponce de León went back to Spain to get permission—and money—from the king to conquer and colonize the land of Florida he had just discovered, in addition to the island of Bimini. He knew they were separate but still believed they were both islands. The Spanish rulers gave their assent in 1514, just one year after Ponce de Léon's discovery. Yet the explorer delayed his trip back to Florida. He was not a young man by then, fifty-four years old, and as Weber quoted him in a letter to a royal official, "My wife has died and I have daughters still, and I have not dared leave them unprotected until they marry."

Some five years later, however, stories about the fabulous riches that Hernando Cortés had gained in his conquest of Mexico's Aztec Empire fired up the imagination of all Europeans, especially that of Ponce de León, who finally decided to embark on his next adventure to Florida, which he had officially discovered.

It took him until 1521 to organize the expedition, as much of the financing was going to explorers headed for places such as Mexico. This time he brought not just soldiers, adventurers, and gold seekers but also priests, farmers, and artisans. Also aboard ship were domestic animals and farming implements. They intended to not just explore Florida but to settle in it. For the site of what he hoped would be the first permanent colony in Florida, Ponce again chose the vicinity of Charlotte Harbor, where Calusa Indians had chased him off eight years earlier.

Ponce de León brought domestic animals, like these horses, on his ships in order to make a permanent settlement in Florida.

Shortly after landing, as the Spaniards began to seek supplies and construct their first buildings, the Calusas attacked again. This time Ponce de León was hit by a poisoned arrow. Then, as they did eight years earlier in the same region, the Spaniards abandoned their attempt to colonize Florida. They sailed to Havana, Cuba, where after a few days Ponce de León died of his injuries. He is buried in the Cathedral of San Juan, Puerto Rico.

Juan Ponce de León went down in history with a mixed reputation. He had a record of treating Native Americans cruelly. He also went to his death still thinking Florida was an island, not a peninsula connected to the North American continent. Yet the story of his search for the Fountain of Youth still fires the imagination. And he still remains the first European known to have set foot in what is now the United States.

WANDERING SPANIARD

Seven years after Ponce de Léon's failed attempt to establish a colony in Florida, another Spanish adventurer, Pánfilo de Narváez, tried again. Like Ponce de Léon, Narváez was inspired to find treasure that matched the riches of Mexico—he had seen them close up when he spent three years there as a prisoner of his bitter rival Cortés.

Narváez's Florida expedition, made up of four hundred men, landed near Tampa Bay in 1528. He quickly made enemies of the local Native Americans, and in an act of great cruelty cut off the nose of Chief Hirrihigua of the Ocita tribe. Perhaps wanting to get rid of Narváez, another Florida tribe, the Timucuan, told him tales of a wealthy city farther north. Narváez decided to split his men up. Some three hundred men would march up the coast with him in search of the city, while the ships would sail north to meet up with Narváez later. Narváez surely envisioned himself filling the ships with gold. But one year later the sailors and soldiers still had not found each other. The men sailing the ships gave up the search and sailed back to a Spanish port. Meanwhile, Narváez was leading his men to the Tallahassee region, where the Timucuans had told him gold was plentiful. The Apalachee Indians who lived there welcomed the bearded strangers at first but attacked the Spaniards after Narváez took a chief hostage and demanded gold for his return. Finding no riches,

Native Americans living in Florida welcomed Pánfilo de Narváez when he arrived in Tallahassee.

and under constant attack by the Apalachee, Narváez eventually gave up his dream of finding wealth. He also realized he was not going to find his ships and figured the expedition could not survive Native American attacks and illness for much longer. He decided the fastest way to reach a safe Spanish harbor was to sail to Mexico along the Gulf Coast. For this purpose his men built five barges from horsehide, ripped their shirts open to use as sails, and set out for Mexico. They made it as far as the Texas coast before a storm sank the barges. Most of the men died, including Narváez himself.

One who survived was Álvar Núñez Cabeza de Vaca. Cabeza de Vaca's survival of the shipwreck was but the beginning of a remarkable story. He spent the next few years lost in the southwestern wilderness, not looking for gold but simply trying to survive. Cabeza de Vaca later wrote a book he called *Naufragios* (Spanish for Shipwrecks) in which he told his amazing tale of survival. It is also the first book-length description of the people, the landscape, and the animals of what centuries later would become the American Southwest.

Cabeza de Vaca was a true survivor. Most of the men who survived the sinking of Narváez's doomed barges eventually separated from one another and died. Cabeza de Vaca managed to locate three other survivors, who stayed with him through his wanderings. (One of them was an African slave named Esteban, who is thought to be the first African to have set foot in what is now the United States.) In a rever-

Cabeza de Vaca wrote about his wanderings. This symbol is from the title page of his book, *Naufragios*.

sal of the usual roles, Native Americans enslaved Cabeza de Vaca and his three companions. At first they went along, on foot, following their Native-American masters. Later, their living conditions began to improve.

Cabeza de Vaca was not like some earlier explorers. He did not treat the Native Americans with the cruelty typical of other conquistadores. Of course, as a slave he was in no position to be harsh—yet his writings indicate a degree of sympathy for the different cultures he encountered. Eventually he and his companions managed to convince the Native Americans that they were miracle healers, even though no one in the group of four knew any medicine. Aside from performing at least one surgical procedure, treatment usually consisted of dramatically making the sign of the cross and praying over a sick Native American.

That seemed to work often enough, because word of their healings spread. Native Americans "would come from many parts to find us, saying we were truly the children of the sun," he wrote in *Naufragios*. Cabeza de Vaca was the most well regarded of the four. "We all came to be like doctors, although as far as daring to attempt any cure I was most often chosen among the others." To Cabeza de Vaca and his Catholic companions, the effectiveness of the prayers in healing the sick was a sign that the God of Christianity supported Spain's efforts to conquer the Americas and convert its inhabitants.

Cabeza de Vaca and his three lonely, lost companions were not able to conquer anybody. They were lucky to survive. As years went by and his fame continued to spread, Cabeza de Vaca became a kind of wandering healer, a performer of miracles who received food, shelter, and gratitude from the Native-American villages he entered. They even began to follow him in his travels, which took a southwesterly route in order to get closer to Spanish settlements in northern Mexico. Finally, in 1536, eight years after his odyssey began, Cabeza de Vaca came upon "four Christians on horseback." They were part of a larger group of Spaniards who took him in.

Cabeza de Vaca returned to Spain, but his adventures were not over yet. In the early 1540s he explored South America, becoming the first European to see the spectacular Iguazú Falls on the Argentina-Brazil border. Again in South America, he gained a reputation for his humane treatment of Native Americans. He eventually returned to Spain and died in the mid–1550s.

CHAPTER THREE

The Big Explorations

T HE EXPEDITIONS OF JUAN PONCE DE LEÓN AND Pánfilo de Narváez were short-lived disasters. Cabeza de Vaca's journey lasted for years, but was far from an organized exploration—it was a battle for survival carried out by four lost men.

Only a short time after Cabeza de Vaca's rescue, however, two conquistadores led organized expeditions that explored much of the United States, even deep inland. Hernando de Soto marched his men through most of the southeastern states. At around the same time, Francisco Vázquez de Coronado was leading his men through the deserts of Arizona and New Mexico into Kansas and the Great Plains. Both expeditions had a similar motivation: to find gold. But they learned that the Native-American tribes of North America had no

Opposite: Hernando de Soto departs from Spain to explore Florida.

material riches to match the fabulous wealth of the Aztec Empire in Mexico. Neither expedition left lasting settlements.

DE SOTO'S OLD—VERY OLD—SOUTH

The first of the two men to hit North American shores was de Soto, who landed on the Gulf Coast of Florida, probably around Tampa Bay, in 1539. It had been more than a decade since Narváez's failed attempt to colonize Florida and just two years since Cabeza de Vaca had stumbled upon the Spaniards who rescued him after his years of wandering. In Spain, de Soto (who had participated in the conquest of Peru and fully understood the difficulties of exploring the New World) tried to recruit the vastly experienced Cabeza de Vaca. But Cabeza de Vaca did not wish to return to Florida.

Hernando de Soto tried to succeed in Florida where other explorers had failed.

The expedition went ahead anyway—one of the largest Spain had mounted up to that time. It had nine ships "with a large number of horses, mules, pigs and dogs, and well over 600 Europeans." Their intent was to find gold in Florida, convert the natives to Christianity, and perhaps start the settlements earlier conquistadores had failed to establish. To the Spanish of the era, however, Florida did not only mean the land that the modern American state encompasses; to Spain, Florida extended from the peninsula that forms today's state of the same name all the way north to Delaware Bay, which is just south of New Jersey.

And that may explain the great geographic extent of de Soto's explorations. Historians do not universally agree about his exact route, but most believe he traveled thousands of miles in a meandering trail that took him from Florida up to North Carolina and then as far west as modern-day Texas.

De Soto's luck was mixed at the start of his journey. One good thing was that he found a survivor of the Narváez expedition, Juan Ortiz, who had been living with Native Americans, and agreed to act as a translator and cultural interpreter. Unfortunately, among the first Native-American chiefs de Soto met after landing in Florida was Hirrihigua, who had never forgotten that another Spaniard—Narváez—had cut off his nose years earlier. Relations between the Native Americans and the Spaniards were tense, and de Soto found no riches. He headed north to continue his exploration, but still found no riches comparable to what his fellow Spaniards had forcibly taken from the Aztecs of Mexico or the Incas of Peru. De Soto had himself seen the vast Inca treasure as a member of the Spanish army that conquered Peru under Francisco Pizarro, so he was unimpressed by the handicrafts he saw during his North American wanderings. The Native Americans were unimpressed by the

did. They were either passing on ancient local traditions or making up stories to get the Spaniards to leave.

It was in northern Alabama that the Spaniards—who up to that point had used their firepower and horses to overwhelm the people they met—were handed their first serious military setback. Near the city of Mabila, one of the largest in the

When the Spaniards reached Alabama, they attacked the Native Americans living in the area.

region, the Choctaw chief Tuscaloosa led an attack on de Soto's men. The Spaniards drove them away, with many casualties on both sides. An enraged de Soto decided to destroy Mabila in revenge. The stockaded settlement was besieged, and when the Spaniards battled their way inside, there was house-to-house fighting for hours. The Spaniards wiped out the large village and killed some 2,500 Native Americans, the historian Miguel Albornoz said. But the

Spanish suffered 30 dead, more than 250 injured, and the loss of 45 horses. The Spanish had won what de Soto considered the greatest battle he had ever fought, but at a great cost to themselves.

The Spanish left the area and headed westward, still looking for that elusive gold. In 1541, de Soto and his men became the first Europeans documented with certainty to have seen the Mississippi River. But after nearly three years

Hernando de Soto is seen here (on white horse), in 1541, discovering the Mississippi River.

of searching for riches and still not finding any gold, some of de Soto's men had become discouraged. They argued that it was time for the expedition to turn south toward the safety of New Spain, in Mexico. The great river before them, they figured, might lead to the Gulf of Mexico and a way home.

De Soto, believing Native-American tales of villages filled with gold, decided to continue wandering through Arkansas, Oklahoma, and Texas. But his discoveries ended in 1542, when de Soto became ill and died. The remnants of his party decided to turn back. They marched over land for four months until they reached the Mississippi River again. Near the present city of Natchez they built rafts to travel the great river into the

A PENINSULA, NOT AN ISLAND

Was Hernando de Soto the first European to reach the Mississippi River? Some historians believe that although he was the first to see it from land, some twenty years earlier another Spanish explorer, Alonso Álvarez de Pineda, charted the great river's mouth, where it empties into the Gulf of Mexico. Álvarez de Pineda explored the Gulf Coast from Florida to Texas. He was the first to show that Florida was not an island but a peninsula on the North American continent.

Gulf of Mexico. After fifty-three days of sailing the Mississippi, they finally reached the Spanish settlement of Pánuco, in Mexico.

Survivors of the de Soto expeditions never found the riches they sought and founded no colonies. The legacy of de Soto's cruel treatment of Native Americans survives to this day, as does his claim to have been the first European to explore the American South, cross its most famous river, and climb its greatest mountain chain.

Hernando de Soto was buried in the Mississippi River after he died in 1542.

A FAILED SETTLEMENT

In their travels across North America, neither de Soto nor Coronado spent a lot of effort trying to establish permanent settlements. That had been tried by Ponce de León a decade earlier, but was stopped by Native-American attacks even before the Spanish had built the first town. Some years later another Spanish adventurer, Lucas Vázquez de Ayllón, fared somewhat better, for a little while.

Vázquez de Ayllón used the fortune he had made in the island of Hispaniola (occupied today by the Dominican Republic and Haiti) to explore the coast of North America. His six vessels landed near the mouth of the South Santee River in what is now South Carolina, but found no gold, little population, and land not suitable for agriculture. He rode south with some of his men and met up again with his ships, in what is present-day Georgia. There, in 1526, he established a town he called San Miguel de Guadalupe. It is considered the first Spanish settlement in the United States. But it failed when disease, hunger, and a harsh winter caused the death of Ayllón and convinced the surviving colonists to leave. Just 150 made it back to Hispaniola. The first permanent settlement would have to wait.

ACROSS THE SOUTHWEST

Just a few months after de Soto landed in Florida, Francisco Vázquez de Coronado led another Spanish expedition across what is now the U.S.-Mexico border and spent the next two years exploring what would become the American Southwest. He journeyed through the high desert of Arizona and New Mexico, crossing the Texas Panhandle into Oklahoma and the plains of Kansas before turning back. At one point, while Coronado was in Kansas, de Soto was just some 300 miles (483 kilometers) away in Arkansas. Although the two expeditions never met up, one Native-American woman was an unfortunate link. She managed to escape a life of slavery among Coronado's men, only to be recaptured by de Soto.

Like so many Spanish explorers of the era, Coronado was a member of the lower nobility out for gold in the New World after an older brother had inherited the family estate. Coronado arrived in Mexico in 1535 and, after a short time, was named the governor of Nueva Galicia, in northwestern Mexico, which was the northernmost Spanish settlement in North America. Back in Mexico City, *Viceroy* Antonio de Mendoza heard stories of a *friar* named Marcos de Niza who claimed to have seen the city of Cíbola, one of the legendary Seven Cities of Gold, larger and richer than even the Aztecs' capital city of Tenochtitlán (which became Mexico City after the Spanish conquest). Some believed de Niza was lying, so Mendoza sent Coronado to see if it was true. Coronado, with his thirst for gold, was happy to oblige.

The expedition was one of the largest up to that point. One historian wrote that it included more than 300 Spaniards, about 1,000 Native Americans, and 1,500 horses and pack animals. They marched along northward, following de Niza, who had come with the expedition to show the way, and crossed from Mexico into what is now the United States. It was there that the explorers' dreams of riches began to shatter. The fabled Cíbola turned out to be an impoverished Zuni Indian village of one hundred families. Coronado was so angry at de Niza that he ordered him to return to Mexico City. "He has not told the truth in a single thing he has said," Weber quoted from a report written by the bitterly disappointed Coronado. "Everything is the opposite of what he related, except the name of the cities and the large stone houses."

Nevertheless, Coronado did not let the disappointment at Cíbola end his dream of finding gold. He made the town his base of operations and sent out a number of scouting parties. One of them, under the leadership of García López de Cárdenas, explored Hopi Indian villages and probably became the first European party to see the magnificent Grand Canyon. Yet as Weber wrote, they saw it as "a formidable obstacle" to their journey rather than "a place of beauty." To sixteenth-century Europeans, Weber noted, "unbridled wildness had little aesthetic appeal."

Other scouting parties explored the country of the Pueblo Indians, around today's Albuquerque. Perhaps

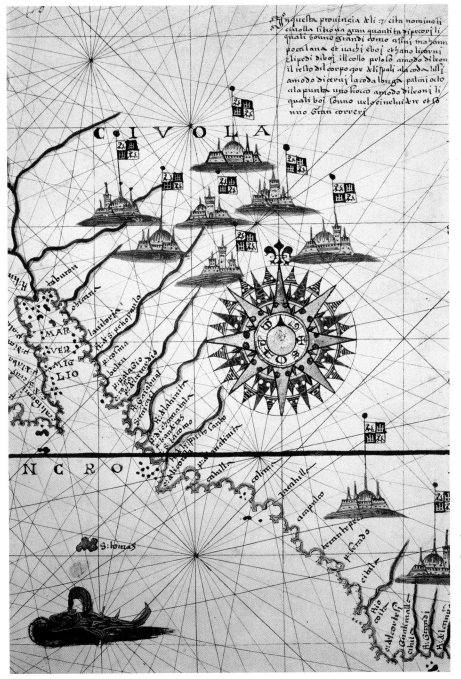

In questa prouincia d'li 7 cita nominali
cibolla si troua gran quantita di ercori li
quali sonno grandi como asini ma hanno
pocula na et uachi eboi ethano licorni
el ipedi dito s' ill collo pelolo amodo di leou
il resto del corpo goe d' li spali ala coda lisi
amodo di cerui la coda buga palmi octo
ala punta uno fioco amodo di leoni li
quali boi sonno uel cinclui der et so
nno gran correri

C I V O L A

M A R
VER
MIG
LIO

taburdu

S: lomas

N C R O

acapulco

The Seven Cities
of Gold sits in the
Kingdom of Cíbola
(also called
Cívola), which are
depicted in this
map from 1567.
Cíbola is in what is
now New Mexico.

THE BIG EXPLORATIONS

43

because Pueblo irrigation techniques made the dry land produce food, Coronado decided to move his headquarters there.

Relations between Coronado's men and the Pueblo quickly turned sour. As winter approached, it became apparent that Pueblo farmers could not sustain both themselves and their unwelcome guests. Supplies of food and clothing began to grow short, and the Spaniards, together with the Native Americans they had brought from Mexico, robbed the Pueblo of their supplies. There were also cases of cruelty that could not be justified by the struggle to survive. Coronado's men torched entire villages and burned inhabitants at the stake. By spring, Weber said, thirteen villages had been destroyed. So it must have been a relief to the surviving Pueblo, many hiding in the mountains, to see Coronado's party leave.

It was, again, the search for fabulously wealthy cities that pushed

ROUTES OF CABEZA DE VACA, CORONADO, AND DE SOTO AND MOSCOSCO*

from Quivira

Coronado's army

Return of Coronado's Army

Coronado's route to Quivira

De Soto's route from the Mabila area in south central Alabama

Cabeza de Vaca's route from Tampa Bay

GULF OF MEXICO

–·–·–·–·— The expedition of Núñez Cabeza de Vaca (1528-1535)

————————— The expedition of Vázquez de Coronado (1540-1542)

— — — — — The expedition of Hernando de Soto
and Luis de Moscoso (1539-1543)

*The routes traveled by the three conquistadores are still in dispute; the routes shown here are the ones accepted by many historians.

Sources: Arthur Grove Day, *Coronado's Quest: The Discovery of the Southwestern States*, University of California Press, 1940; Cleve Hallenbeck, *Álvar Núñez Cabeza de Vaca: The Journey and Route of the First European to Cross the Continent of North America, 1534-1536*, Arthur H. Clark Company, Glendale, California, 1940; George Parker Winship, ed., *The Journey of Coronado: 1540-1542*, Allerton Book Company, New York, 1922; U.S. De Soto Expedition Commission, *Final Report of the United States De Soto Expedition Commission* (76th Congress, 1st. Session, House Document No. 71, 1939). Base map adapted from Erwin Raisz, "Landforms of the United States," 1957 and "Landforms of Mexico," 1964.

The routes of Spanish explorers Álvar Núñez Cabeza de Vaca, Francisco Vázquez de Coronado, and Hernando de Soto are seen here.

the Spaniards on. This time the city was named Quivira. A Native American whom Coronado's men called the Turk told Coronado that Quivira was to the north of Pueblo country and that it was so rich, "the common table service of all was generally wrought silver, and . . . the pitchers, dishes and bowls were made of gold," as one historian wrote.

Coronado and his men followed the Turk on a wild trek across the rest of New Mexico, into Texas and Oklahoma. They reached as far east as central Kansas. Having found nothing they valued, they turned against the Turk in frustration. "Where is the Quivira you told us about," they demanded. Weber said the Native American confessed it had all been a ruse to get the Spaniards out of Pueblo country into unknown lands, where they might starve. The Turk was executed, and the disappointed Spaniards began a long march home without any gold. They reentered Spanish Mexico in 1542, about the same time that survivors of de Soto's expedition had returned by way of the sea after their own failed quest for gold.

Coronado, unlike de Soto, survived his journey. Upon returning to Mexico, Coronado was investigated for mismanaging the expedition, but no charges were filed. Like de Soto, he left no permanent settlements. Both men will be remembered for their cruelty to the Native Americans they met, as well as for producing the first written descriptions of a huge swath of what would become the United States—from Florida to the Carolinas to the Mississippi River, and through the southern Midwest into Texas and into the deserts of Arizona.

A statue of Francisco Vázquez de Coronado stands today in New Mexico.

CHAPTER FOUR

SETTLING FLORIDA

IN THE YEARS AFTER COLUMBUS MADE HIS first landfall in the New World, Spain conquered the powerful empires of the Inca in Peru and the Aztec in Mexico, and established large colonial cities from the Caribbean to South America. Yet to the north, in what is now the United States, attempts to form permanent settlements continued to fail. For nearly three quarters of a century after Columbus landed, no European nation—not Great Britain, not France, not even Spain, the superpower of the age—was able to establish a lasting colony north of the Rio Grande.

It was not for lack of trying. Apart from the famous but ultimately fruitless explorations by de Soto and Coronado, and apart from the battles for survival of Ponce de León as well as Cabeza de Vaca, a number of lesser-known explorers also tried to create permanent settlements.

Opposite: Tristán de Luna set out from Mexico to explore the interior of North America.

49

Among them was Tristán de Luna. By 1559, when his expedition set out from Veracruz, Mexico, the travels of Coronado and de Soto had made Florida and the interior of North America more familiar to Europeans. Spaniards had an idea about the region's rivers, mountains, and coastlines as well as more knowledge about the Native Americans who lived there. But nations such as Great Britain and France had also learned from the Spanish expeditions, as well as from some of their own explorers. They became Spain's rivals in the race to build empires in the New World, and the Spanish king Felipe II (also known as Philip II) considered it his job to beat them. Luna was given the mission of establishing a permanent Spanish presence to keep out the British and French.

The plan was to build a town on the Gulf of Mexico and from there conquer for Spain a territory that stretched all the way to coastal South Carolina. There was great hope for success—de Luna was a veteran of the Coronado expedition, and he took with him five veterans of the de Soto expedition, men who were already familiar with part of the route they were to travel. Things began well, with the construction of the city they named Santa María de Filipino as a base on Pensacola Bay. But after a hurricane and food shortages, the Spanish moved inland to find the Native-American farming communities de Soto had reported years before. The Native Americans remembered the Spanish cruelty of a generation earlier and offered the newcomers no help.

While de Luna and his men struggled to survive at Santa María, the Spanish king learned that the French were planning to build a settlement on the Atlantic coast and ordered de Luna to get there first. De Luna sent one party on a ship, around the Florida peninsula, but it was wrecked in a storm. Another group tried to make its way by land but miscalculated the distance and only got halfway to the coast, to near the area where de Soto had fought a pitched battle with Native Americans decades earlier. In 1561 de Luna was relieved of his duties, and Santa María was abandoned.

FINALLY, SAINT AUGUSTINE

Yet Felipe II knew he could not give up and abandon North America to the French or British. Even if the region could not match the gold and silver the Spaniards were taking out of Mexico and Peru, a lasting Spanish presence was necessary to fight rival European powers. In Felipe's view, Spain needed to build permanent colonies in North America to control not just the land, but also the sea lanes Spain used to trade with its established outposts in Mexico, the Caribbean, and South America.

He put the task in the hands of Pedro Menéndez de Avilés, a wealthy nobleman who had reached a high rank in the Spanish navy.

The travels of Pedro Menendez de Aviles were recognized in 1960 by Spain with a postage stamp bearing his image.

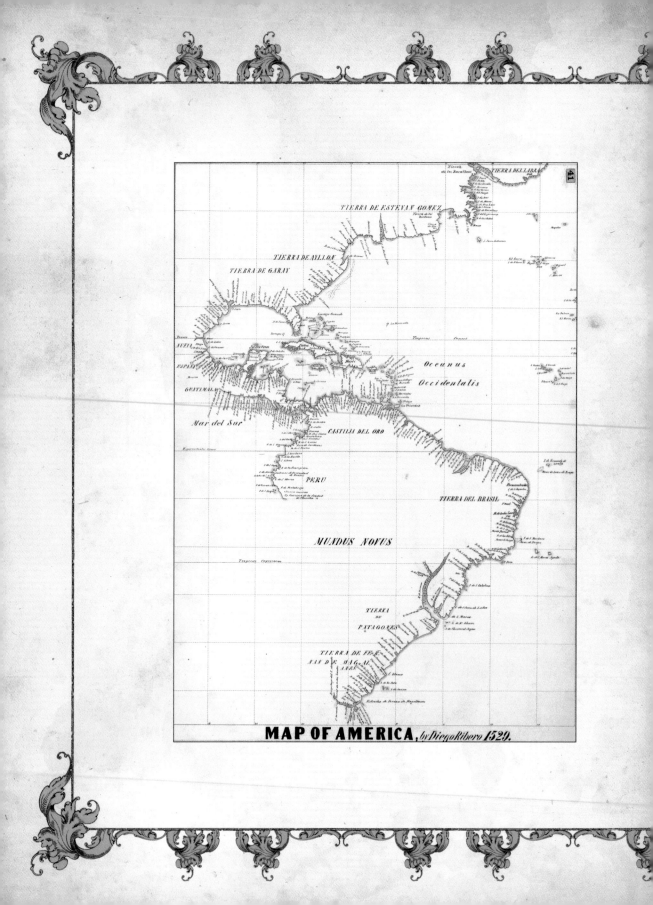

MAP OF AMERICA, by Diego Ribero 1529.

SEARCH FOR THE NORTHERN PASSAGE

When Esteban Gómez, a Portuguese sailor in the service of Spain, set out for North America, he was not looking for gold or to establish a colony. What he wanted to find was the *Northern Passage* to Asia. As part of the Ferdinand Magellan expedition that was first to *circumnavigate* the world, he knew firsthand what a perilous journey it was to reach Asia—which the Europeans were trying to reach for its coveted silk and spices—by sailing around the tip of South America, with its intensely stormy seas. Gómez hoped Asia could be reached more easily if he found a sea route to the north of the New World.

Some historians believe he began his search for the Northern Passage in Florida, from which he made his way up the coast, as far north as Nova Scotia, Canada. A true man of the sea, he never went much inland along his route. Yet he charted bays, beaches, and peninsulas that he saw from his ship in regions of North America not usually associated with Spanish exploration—Delaware Bay, New York Harbor, Cape Cod. At least two towns in coastal Maine, Casco and Saco, today retain the names given to them by Gómez for the shape of their bays—Casco had the outline of a helmet, and Saco looked to Gómez like a sack.

Gómez never did find the Northern Passage, but his explorations resulted in the creation of one of the first accurate maps of America's eastern seaboard, drawn in 1529, and showing the New England states as "Land of Estevan Gómez."

Menéndez sailed out of the Spanish port of Cádiz with one thousand men in three ships, and on September 8, 1565, landed in a harbor on the central Atlantic coast of Florida, near where the Spanish believed France had built a settlement named Fort Caroline. With the usual pomp of unfurling banners, trumpets, and upraised crosses, he took possession of the land for Spain. Menéndez proclaimed that at that site he would establish a settlement named for the Catholic saint on whose feast day he had first sighted the harbor, Saint

The town of Saint Augustine, Florida was named after the Catholic saint of the same name.

Augustine. Today at that same site is the Florida city of Saint Augustine. It has been continuously inhabited since the Menéndez landing—forty-two years before the first permanent English settlement in Jamestown and fifty-five years before the Pilgrims arrived at Plymouth Rock. Saint Augustine is the first permanent European settlement on American soil. In other words, it is the oldest city of European origin in the United States.

Right from the start, Menéndez and his men faced trouble. They had barely begun to build fortifications when three French ships were sighted off the harbor. A storm drove the

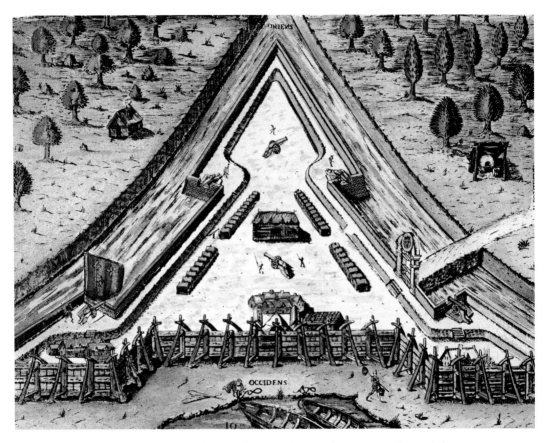

vessels south, preventing their planned attack on the Spanish. Menéndez reacted quickly. Knowing that most of the French soldiers were probably aboard those ships, Menéndez ordered his men to march north 40 miles (64.4 kilometers), even while the storm was still blowing, and attack Fort Caroline. Because the French were Protestants who had left France to flee religious persecution, the Catholic Spaniards saw them not only as colonial rivals but also as *heretics*. They showed no mercy. Women and children were spared, but most of the men of Fort Caroline were massacred.

Fort Caroline was built by the French in 1564 as an experimental community for French Protestants to practice their religion freely.

AS FAR AS THEY GOT

Shortly after his arrival at Saint Augustine, Menéndez sent a trusted aide named Juan Pardo to protect Spanish seafarers and trade along the Atlantic coast and to blaze a trail to the rich Spanish colonies in Mexico.

After building the first settlement at Santa Elena, in present-day South Carolina, Pardo set out to expand the Spanish presence in the area. But like de Luna some years earlier, he vastly underestimated the distance between the Carolinas and Mexico, and his men spent time lost in unfamiliar lands with unfriendly Native Americans. The question that has long interested historians is how far they got. One possible answer is that they got at least as far as the region near Asheville, North Carolina, where archaeologists digging in a farm field recently found ruins and artifacts at what they think is the former site of a Spanish fort named San Juan, which lasted from 1566 to 1568.

Menéndez renamed the fort San Mateo and marched south again to look for the French ships. Most of the ships had been destroyed in the storm so he captured hundreds of shipwreaked sailors some 18 miles (29 km) below Saint Augustine. Once again he ordered the majority of the men executed. He reported it all to the king, noting that he had done away with members of the "evil Lutheran sect." It had been mere weeks since Menéndez's landing, and already he had gone a long way toward accomplishing his mission of wiping out Spain's imperial rivals in the region.

A view overlooking the town of Saint Augustine, Florida.

Within the year, Menéndez had built a string of five Atlantic coast fortifications that stretched from present-day downtown Miami to Santa Elena, on what is now the Marine base at Parris Island, South Carolina. On Florida's Gulf Coast he built one fort at Tampa Bay and another at Charlotte Harbor—as if to tell the Calusa Indians, who had driven away Ponce de León from that very same place some fifty years earlier, that the Spanish had come back to stay.

But at Saint Augustine, even though it was the main settlement, staying was not easy. For one thing, the land was inhospitable. The area was, as quoted by one contemporary account, "all a forest . . . so filled with roots that it cannot be cultivated except a part that is sandy." Little other than corn and squash would grow. Nor was there much land fit for raising livestock—the herds of pigs and cattle brought from Spain could not multiply because their newborns would starve to death or be eaten by bears or cougars. Settlers eked out a meager existence, surviving mostly on the few crops they raised and what they caught from the sea.

They had housing problems, too. Rainy weather and salty air rotted away the timber-framed buildings, few of which lasted for more than four or five years. The Spaniards spent just about every waking moment farming, grinding their grain, or fixing buildings that were falling apart—from people's homes to the main fort.

"Despite all this, many months they do not give them rations nor pay," wrote the same contemporary observer. "Beset by hunger and nakedness, they have wanted to leave. But because they have no way to go by land nor ship to go by sea, they have not gone."

And that was when things were peaceful. The colonists also had to survive attacks by Native Americans and colonial rivals. Timucua Indians from Seloy burned down much of Saint Augustine barely eight months after it was first built, while Menéndez and a force of soldiers were away exploring. When he returned, he moved the settlement across the bay to Anastasia Island and built a new fort. That one rotted after a few years, and by the time the English *privateer* Francis Drake attacked the settlement, now back on the main land, in 1586, the Spaniards were in their sixth fort.

Drake had two thousand fighting men with him, at a time when Saint Augustine's population was about three hundred. The English burned everything in sight and nearly killed off the young Spanish colony. By then only Saint Augustine and Santa Elena hundreds of miles to the north remained of the string of fortresses Menéndez had built. Santa Elena was abandoned in 1587, its inhabitants moving to Saint Augustine. And there they held on, supplied by Havana politically and economically because the Spanish crown had decided it needed to keep a toehold on the Atlantic coast of America, north of Mexico.

Sir Francis
Drake was the
first Englishman
to sail around
the world.

Saint Augustine remained in Spanish hands until 1821, except from 1763 to 1783, when it was under British rule. In 1821, when the young United States bought from Spain what was to become the state of Florida. By that time it was clear that Spain's sixteenth-century dream of having an empire that stretched from Florida through eastern North America would not be fulfilled. Spain governed Florida in name only. In reality, it controlled little beyond Saint Augustine. In western North America, however, Spain was much more successful.

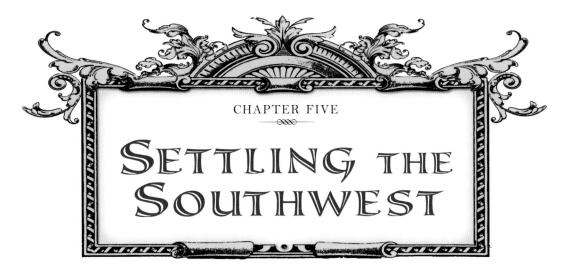

CHAPTER FIVE

SETTLING THE SOUTHWEST

THE FOUNDING OF SAINT AUGUSTINE WAS A reminder that Felipe II felt it was imperative to build a string of outposts from Florida to the Carolinas to defend against British and French incursions. But when it came to the opposite side of the North American continent, Spain's monarch reached the opposite conclusion: Do not worry about it.

By the mid-1570s no European rival disputed the Spanish dominance of the Pacific Ocean, where its ships traveled from the Philippines to South America. As to the interior West and Southwest of what is now the United States, there were no worries there, either. Spain had complete control of the land routes, all of which led out of Mexico, which had been firmly in the hands of Spain since Cortés's conquest of the Aztecs

Opposite:
The Spanish were dominant in the Pacific Ocean, where they often fought other passing ships. Here, the Spanish treasure ship *Nuestra Senora de la concepcion* engages in combat with Sir Francis Drake's ship, *Golden Hind.*

half a century earlier. Besides, there was not a lot of interest in the region, because earlier explorations had found none of the riches the conquistadores had taken in the much wealthier Mexico. The biggest exploration of all, Coronado's search for the legendary Seven Cities of Gold, had turned up nothing but a handful of small Native-American villages.

Still, hope died hard among the *hidalgos* who dreamed of glory, treasure, and the spread of Catholicism. The Spanish population of Mexico was spreading north with the additional discovery of silver mines, and by the early 1580s Spaniards were back exploring the area north of the Rio Grande for the first time since Coronado and de Soto. Among those explorers were Antonio de Espejo and a Franciscan friar named Agustín Rodríguez. Each man traveled separately several hundred miles into the territory of the Pueblo Indians, who lived in multistory dwellings and had one of the most advanced civilizations north of Mexico. Rodríguez named the region San Felipe del Nuevo México. The Spanish word *nuevo*, meaning new, distinguished the region from the old Mexico that Spain had controlled for two generations.

SPANIARDS IN NEW MEXICO
The man Felipe II chose to lead the Spanish effort to colonize western North America was Juan de Oñate Salazar, born into an aristocratic family in Zacatecas, Mexico—

one of the first conquistadores born in the New World. Still, the king hesitated to give him full support. "This discovery and pacification is to be accomplished without spending or pledging anything from my treasury," Felipe II insisted. But Oñate had enough of his own money to finance the expedition, in the hope of winning more riches and fame. "I shall give your majesty a new world, greater than New Spain," he wrote. Oñate and his expedition (of 500 people, including 130 soldiers) forded the Rio Grande at the site of present-day El Paso in 1598 and marched through the land of the Pueblos until he reached a settlement called Yungue. He took it over, built a church, and renamed it San Gabriel. It was to be Oñate headquarters, and the major Spanish outpost in the Southwest.

From San Gabriel, Oñate sent expeditions all around the area. He wanted to find a route to the Pacific and to contact Spanish possessions on the Atlantic. His parties reached the Texas Panhandle, the Gulf of California, and perhaps as far northeast as Kansas. But none of them found what they were looking for. The technology of the time enabled people to accurately measure distances north and south, but not east and west. So like the majority of his contemporaries, Oñate badly misjudged the width of the North American continent. He believed both coasts were much closer to his base in New Mexico than they actually were.

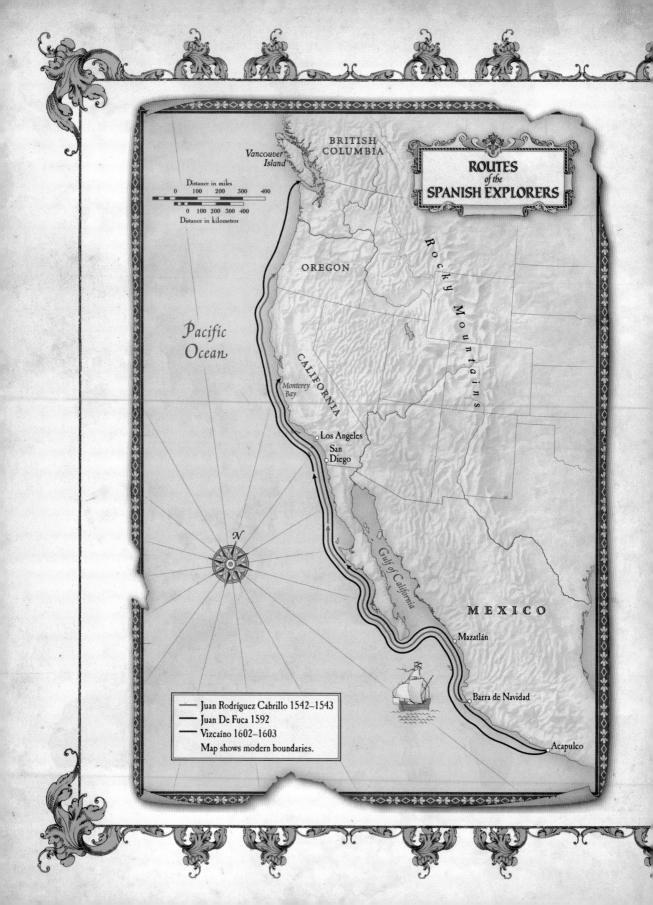

BRITISH
COLUMBIA

*Vancouver
Island*

*Pacific
Ocean*

OREGON

Rocky Mountains

CALIFORNIA

*Monterey
Bay*

Los Angeles
San
Diego

Gulf of California

MEXICO

Mazatlán

Barra de Navidad

Acapulco

N

Distance in miles
0   100   200   300   400
0   100 200 300 400
Distance in kilometers

ROUTES
of the
SPANISH EXPLORERS

—— Juan Rodríguez Cabrillo 1542–1543
—— Juan De Fuca 1592
—— Vizcaíno 1602–1603
   Map shows modern boundaries.

PACIFIC EXPLORATIONS

Although the Pacific coast of North America was not a top priority of Spain's colonial efforts in the 1500s and 1600s, at least three expeditions left their mark in the region. The first was led by Juan Rodríguez Cabrillo. His three ships left the Pacific port of Barra de Navidad, Mexico, in 1542 and headed north into waters never before sailed by Europeans. The expedition anchored at what would become the harbors of San Diego and Los Angeles, where the Spaniards heard Native Americans tell tales of armed, bearded men roaming the interior, murdering and pillaging—probably the Coronado party. Eventually, the Native Americans attacked. Cabrillo died from an infection after falling on slippery rocks during one battle. The expedition continued as far as the California-Oregon border before turning back.

Some historians believe Juan de Fuca went even farther north fifty years later, perhaps as far as British Columbia. His goal was to find the elusive Northern Passage that connected the Atlantic and Pacific oceans. Most explorers of the era tried to find it by sailing from east to west, but de Fuca tried sailing from west to east. De Fuca never found it, but he did claim to have discovered a broad inlet that some historians believe is the strait that today bears his name, which separates Vancouver Island from the mainland.

Another Pacific exploration, led by Sebastián Vizcaíno, came about as a result of increased attacks by English ships on Spanish treasure galleons in the Pacific. From 1602 to 1603, Vizcaíno mapped the same coasts Cabrillo had explored six decades earlier and urged that a base be built on Monterey Bay. But it would be decades before Europeans settled California.

The Acoma village in New Mexico, where the Acoma first welcomed the Spaniards, still stands today.

Back at headquarters, there was trouble, too. The Acomas, a peaceful tribe of people who had at first welcomed the Spaniards, became hostile after "soldier-settlers extorted corn, beans, squash and clothing from the Pueblos, resorting to torture, murder and rape," as one historian wrote. Native Americans in the high *mesa*-top Acoma pueblo rebelled, killing close to a dozen Spaniards, including Oñate's nephew. The Spaniards counterattacked, and after a battle that lasted three days, they killed five hundred men and three hundred women and children. Oñate then ordered that captured males older than twenty-five have one foot severed. The controversy surrounding this slaughter lives on in recent times because activists cut off the foot of an Oñate statue during New Mexico's celebration in 1998 of the four-hundredth anniversary of his arrival.

Other Native-American uprisings followed, and were also put down with cruelty. There were additional failed expeditions and more reports of riches that turned out to be false. Colonists started abandoning New Mexico for an easier life in New Spain. By 1607 so many things had gone wrong that Oñate resigned his office. In 1608 he was ordered to go to Mexico City and later faced accusations of using excessive force during the Acoma rebellion. He was never allowed to return to New Mexico.

For the next few years the colony Oñate had started in New Mexico grew faster than the Florida settlement, yet remained small compared to the Spanish dominions in Mexico, the Caribbean, and South America. Its population

Santa Fe houses the San Miguel Church, built in 1610.

was about three thousand people throughout most of the 1600s, "twice the size of Florida but still a modest number," one historian wrote. New Mexico's biggest city, the Villa Real de la Santa Fé, was founded in 1610 by Pedro de Peralta, Oñate's successor. It is second only to Saint Augustine as one of the oldest continuously in-habited city of European origin in the United States and remains the heart of colonial Spanish North America. Santa Fe's Palace of the Governors and its San Miguel Chapel, both constructed shortly after the city's founding, are among the oldest buildings in the country and are classic examples of Spanish colonial architecture.

EXPANSION AND DECLINE

The same year that Santa Fe was founded, English colonists finally managed to establish a permanent colony in North America, at Jamestown, Virginia. Farther north and thirteen years later, the Pilgrims established themselves in Massachusetts. Spain, for all its military might at the time, could not dislodge them. Instead, English colonists soon populated the eastern seaboard from Georgia to Maine—seeds that formed the base for what would become the United States.

Meanwhile, Spain's attempt to colonize North America never quite succeeded, at least not to the ambitious extent the early conquistadores imagined. "Born in dreams of transcontinental empires in North America, the two colonies [of Florida and New Mexico] hung on through much of the seventeenth century as little more than the precarious towns of Santa Fe and Saint Augustine," Weber wrote. Not until the early 1700s did Spain expand its North American holdings, with the building of missions and the founding of towns as far west from Florida as California. One reason for the slow growth is that Florida and the Southwest were not the first choices for Spaniards who sought their fortunes in the New World. The gold and silver of the ruined Aztec and Inca empires beckoned, as did the

opportunities in well-established cities such as Lima, Peru, Havana, Cuba, and Mexico City.

Modern day Saint Augustine.

In short, Great Britain concentrated its colonial efforts in North America, where in 1776 the thirteen colonies would rebel against British rule and form the United States. Meanwhile, Spain focused its colonial efforts in Mexico, the Caribbean, and South America—colonies that, in the early 1800s, rebelled and eventually formed the nations of modern-day Latin America. It is the latter, of course, that have the deeper Spanish legacy. Yet in the United States, too, those Spaniards of long ago and their descendants left a legacy that endures.

TIMELINE

1492	Columbus discovers America.
1513	Juan Ponce de León becomes first European known to have set foot in what is now the United States.
1521	Ponce de León dies on his second trip to the Americas.
1524	Esteban Gómez explores the New England coast.
1526	Lucas Vázquez de Ayllón establishes San Miguel de Guadalupe in Georgia, the earliest known Spanish settlement, which is soon abandoned.
1528	Álvar Núñez Cabeza de Vaca is shipwrecked and begins his eight-year odyssey wandering lost from Florida to Texas.
1539	Hernando de Soto lands in Florida and explores as far as North Carolina and west to Texas; the same year, Francisco Vázquez de Coronado crosses from Mexico into Arizona and explores Texas and Kansas. They are the first Europeans to visit those regions.
1542	De Soto and Coronado expeditions end; Juan Rodríguez Cabrillo explores the California coast, the first European to do so.
1559	Tristán de Luna leads a failed effort to build Spanish colonies in Florida.
1565	Pedro Menéndez de Avilés founds Saint Augustine, the first permanent European colony in what is now the United States; he builds five other settlements, including Santa Elena in Parris Island, South Carolina.
1582	Antonio de Espejo and Agustin Rodríguez explore New Mexico; they are the first Europeans there since Coronado's expedition.
1587	Santa Elena is abandoned; Spanish colonists focus on Florida.
1598	Juan de Oñate crosses into New Mexico and establishes settlement of San Gabriel, which is later abandoned.
1607	First settlement on the site of what in 1610 officially became Santa Fe, the second oldest permanent Spanish settlement after Saint Augustine; in Virginia, English colonists found Jamestown, the first permanent English settlement in the Americas.

GLOSSARY

adelantado Military office of sixteenth-and seventeenth-century Spain under which noblemen received from the monarch permission to govern a territory in exchange for exploring it, settling it, and if necessary, conquering it by force; literally, Spanish for advance man.

Bering Strait Narrow body of water that separates Alaska from Siberia, which in centuries past were connected via a land bridge over which the ancestors of Native Americans migrated from Asia to North America.

circumnavigate To sail around the world.

conquistadores Spanish for conquerors, specifically applied to the men who conquered the Native peoples living in the Americas in the 1500s.

friar Member of a Roman Catholic religious order who takes a vow of poverty and performs community service.

heretic One who deviates from the mainstream teachings of a religion.

hidalgo A member of Spain's lower nobility; a contraction of *hijo de algo*, "son of something."

litter A framework of cloth stretched between two parallel bars for the transportation of a person; a stretcher.

mesa Spanish word for table; also used to mean a high, flat-topped piece of land.

mission One of a series of outposts established by Spanish authorities in California and the Southwest to serve as centers of administration as well as bases from which to convert Native Americans to Catholicism.

moorish Relating to the Moors, the Arab Muslims who ruled parts of Spain between 711 and 1492.

Northern Passage The sea route above the North American continent connecting the Atlantic and Pacific oceans.

privateer A person authorized by a government to rob the treasure ships of rival countries.

rejuvenate To make young again.

viceroy A Spanish royal official who governed a colony as the representative of the monarchy.

western hemisphere North, Central, and South America.

Further Information

Books

Hubbard-Brown, Janet. *Hernando De Soto and His Expeditions Across the Americas* (Explorers of New Lands). New York: Chelsea House, 2005.

McIntosh, Kenneth. *First Encounters Between Spain and the Americas: Two Worlds Meet* (Hispanic Heritage). Broomall, PA: Mason Crest, 2005.

Stein, R. Conrad. *The Conquistadors: Building a Spanish Empire in the Americas* (Proud Heritage). Mankato, MN: Child's World, 2004.

Wulffson, Don. *Before Columbus: Early Voyages to the Americas.* CT: Twenty-First Century Books, 2007.

Web Sites

Cantos Para Todos
www.cantos.org/consult/Onate.html
> A compilation of newspaper articles about the controversy over the four-hundredth anniversary of Juan de Oñate's arrival in and settlement of New Mexico

Catholic Encyclopedia
www.newadvent.org/cathen/12228a.htm
> A biography of Ponce de León

The Hernando de Soto Historical Society
www.desotohq.com
> The official Web site of the Hernando de Soto Historical Society

Public Broadcasting Service
www.pbs.org/weta/thewest/people/a_c/coronado.htm
> Public television documentary *The West*, with information on Francisco Vázquez de Coronado's expedition

Texas State University
www.library.txstate.edu/swwc/cdv/about/index.html
> Cabeza de Vaca's own story about his travails lost in the American wilderness

University of Florida
http://web.uflib.ufl.edu/ufdc/?s=teachers+m=hitplans
> Educational games about Spanish Florida

PLACES TO VISIT

Santa Fe is home to a historic plaza bounded by the Palace of the Governors, whose construction began in 1610, and the Museum of Fine Arts. Across the Santa Fe River and near the New Mexico state capitol is Mission San Miguel, one of the earliest built by the Spanish. On the other side of town, a visitor can see the Museum of Spanish Colonial Art. Check out the visitor's guide at www.santafe.org/.

Although little remains in Saint Augustine from the Spanish colonial era, the imposing **Castillo San Marcos** still stands. Today it is a national monument, and a visitor's guide can be found at www.nps.gov/casa/.

The oldest mission in California, **San Diego de Alcalá** was founded in 1769 by Father Junípero Serra, who also founded a string of missions along the coast, as far west as Sonoma. For background and a visitor's guide, check out www.missionsandiego.com/.

El Alamo is famous in American history for the battle fought there between Mexicans and Texans in 1836. But the building was by then already a century old, founded as Mission San Antonio de Valero. Its official Web site is at www.thealamo.org.

BIBLIOGRAPHY

Albornoz, Miguel. *Hernando de Soto, Knight of the Americas*. New York: Franklin Watts, 1986.

Kessell, John L. *Spain in the Southwest: A Narrative History of Colonial New Mexico, Arizona, Texas, and California*. Norman, OK: University of Oklahoma Press, 2003.

Manucy, Albert. *Sixteenth Century Saint Augustine: The People and Their Homes*. Gainesville, FL: University Press of Florida, 1997.

Weber, David J. *The Spanish Frontier in North America*. New Haven, CT: Yale University Press, 1992.

INDEX

About the Author

ROGER E. HERNÁNDEZ writes a nationally syndicated column distributed by King Features to some forty daily newspapers across the country. He is also Writer in Residence at the New Jersey Institute of Technology and author of *Cubans in America*. Hernández was born in Cuba and came to the United States as a child in 1965, when his parents fled the Castro regime.